D0628026

A Cry for Action

Program Consultants

Stephanie Abraham Hirsh, Ph.D.
Associate Director
National Staff Development Council
Dallas, Texas

Louise Matteoni, Ph.D.
Professor of Education
Brooklyn College
City University of New York

Karen Tindel Wiggins
Social Studies Consultant
Richardson Independent School District
Richardson, Texas

Renee Levitt
Educational Consultant
Scarsdale, New York

STECK-VAUGHN
C O M P A N Y
A Subsidiary of National Education Corporation

MOMENTS IN AMERICAN HISTORY

A Cry for Action

BY
Melissa Stone

Steck-Vaughn Literature Library
Moments in American History

RISKING IT ALL
REBELLION'S SONG
CREATIVE DAYS
RACING TO THE WEST
YOU DON'T OWN ME!
CLOUDS OF WAR
A CRY FOR ACTION
LARGER THAN LIFE
FLYING HIGH
BRIGHTER TOMORROWS

Illustrations: Ron Himler: pp. 8-9, 10, 12, 14-15, 17, 19; Konrad Hack: pp. 20-21, 22, 25, 26, 29, 31; Lyle Miller: cover art, pp. 32-33, 35, 37, 38-39, 41, 43; Linda Graves: pp. 44-45, 46, 49, 50, 53, 55; Steve Cieslawski: pp. 56-57, 59, 60-61, 63, 65, 67; D.J. Simison: pp. 68-69, 70, 73, 75, 76, 79.

Project Editor: Anne Souby

Design: Kirchoff/Wohlberg, Inc.

ISBN 0-8114-4081-8 (pbk.)
ISBN 0-8114-2671-8 (lib. bdg.)   LC 89-110890

Copyright © 1989 Steck-Vaughn Company.
All rights reserved. No part of the material protected by this copyright may be reproduced or utilized in any form or by any means, electronic or mechanical, including photocopying, recording, or by any information storage and retrieval system, without permission in writing from the copyright owner. Requests for permission to make copies of any part of the work should be mailed to: Copyright Permissions, Steck-Vaughn Company, P.O. Box 26015, Austin, Texas 78755.

Printed in the United States of America.

2 3 4 5 6 7 8 9 0 UN 98 97 96 95 94

SKIDMORE COLLEGE LIBRARY

CONTENTS

1870

◄ **ANNIE OAKLEY**
Little Sure Shot, she could
hit any target and blast
every bull's-eye.
(1867-1885)

JOSEPH MCCOY ►
He created an entire town
on the prairie to serve
his booming cattle trade.
(1867)

JANE ADDAMS ►
Her Hull House shone as a
beacon of hope to the poor
people around it.
(1882-1889)

1900

GERONIMO
Driven from his homeland,
this Apache warrior made a
last desperate attempt at
freedom.
(1883-1886)

◄ F.E. AND F.O. STANLEY
Creative inventors, they
used steam to power their
early motor cars.
(1896-1906)

◄ WILLIAM GORGAS
By taking the sting
out of yellow fever,
he made it possible
for workers to complete
the Panama Canal.
(1904-1905)

GERONIMO
THE LAST GREAT APACHE WARRIOR

I am Geronimo, leader of the Chiricahua Apaches! I was not meant to live on a reservation. That is for farmers. I am a warrior. I am free. I will stay free! Many times the soldiers have tricked my people. They promise peace, but give us only capture and death. Our ways are ancient, as old as the world. We cannot change. We must stay free!

G ERONIMO sat alone high on a rocky peak in the Sierra Madre mountains in Mexico in 1883. He surveyed his tribe, the Chiricahua, camped in the narrow valley below.

"This is a good place," Geronimo thought contentedly. "Here we can live much as we did in our ancient tribal lands in Arizona. Here no one tells us how to live — no one tries to force us onto reservations. We are not animals to be penned in and ruled by others!"

Geronimo thought angrily of the time all the Apache tribes had been forced onto the San Carlos reservation in eastern Arizona. After a year of misery, Geronimo had escaped with 74 members of his tribe.

"We are safe here," he thought as he gazed at the deep canyons and rocky cliffs. "No army scout could ever find us."

Geronimo drew the army's attention, however. He sent warriors into Arizona. They raided ranches and stole cattle. They often killed the settlers and burned their farms.

Geronimo approved of this violence against the settlers. "They are our enemies. They take our land. They kill our people. For every Chiricahua they kill, we will kill many more of them."

But inwardly Geronimo sighed in despair. He knew his people were greatly outnumbered. "For every ten we kill, one hundred more take their place," his friend Cochise had said, and it was true.

In Arizona, panic and outrage spread throughout the territory. Newspaper headlines demanded the capture of the outlaw Apaches.

From Washington, D.C., the federal government sent an order to General George Crook at San Carlos: Capture Geronimo!

General Crook knew what a difficult task he faced. He understood Geronimo and the ancient ways of his people.

"Apache boys spend years training to be warriors in these desert mountains," Crook explained to Lieutenant Davis, his aide. "By the time they're men, they can scale vertical cliffs and travel 70 miles a day on foot. Their camps are well hidden — almost impossible to find."

"How will we ever catch them?" asked Davis.

"I don't know. The Apaches know this territory better than anyone," Crook replied. He paused, deep in thought. "That gives me an idea. Maybe it takes an Apache to find an Apache. Some of the reservation Apaches might be willing to help us," he said. "Many of them were Geronimo's rivals."

General Crook's idea was a good one. The Apache men on the reservation were bored and restless. Those who had no relatives with Geronimo agreed to become scouts. Soon Crook had 193 Indian scouts to lead his 2,000 men. They searched for Geronimo's hide-out in the Sierra Madre mountains.

GERONIMO felt safe in his mountain hide-out. He was sure that the army troops could never find him. So he was stunned to see hundreds of U.S. soldiers approaching his camp. It was too late to run. There were too many troops, and his people were too widely scattered.

"You must come to the reservation," Crook announced. "If you come peacefully, you will be treated well. If not, you will all be killed."

As Geronimo faced General Crook, he felt all the muscles in his chest tighten. He wanted to grab a rifle and shoot this enemy.

"What right do you have to come here?" he demanded. "What right do you have to walk on Apache ground?"

"I am here to keep you from killing more settlers," Crook said. "I am here to end your raiding and offer you a peaceful future. If you resist me, the United States Army will hunt your people until you are conquered."

Geronimo said nothing. He knew that the United States Army was much bigger than his band of warriors. He knew that they could not defeat General Crook's troops. Like a mountain lion backed into a cave, he longed to attack. But he knew it was no use. To resist now would mean the senseless death of all his people.

"I must meet with my warriors," he said at last.

General Crook agreed. Geronimo took his warriors aside.

"What choice do we have?" asked one brave. "With Apache scouts working for them, they can find us anywhere."

"We have no place left to hide," said another.

Sadly, Geronimo agreed to bring his tribe back to the San Carlos reservation.

BY the spring of 1884, Geronimo had led most of his followers back to the reservation. Many tried to adjust to the new way of life. They planted gardens and dug irrigation ditches. They stood in line for their meager weekly rations of flour and meat. They tried to get used to staying in one place and giving up their old way of life.

But a year later, Geronimo was still miserable.

"I am a warrior, not a farmer," he said in disgust to a friend, Kaywaykla. He surveyed the barren, gravelly land in front of him. "They give us land, then take away the best parts. They say we can't drink tiswin, the beer we make from corn. They say we can't discipline our families according to Apache customs. They want us to be like children. They want us to live by their rules and customs!"

"Perhaps we have no choice. Perhaps we must learn to accept what we cannot change," Kaywaykla replied.

"I will never accept this life. I am an Apache warrior!" Geronimo declared.

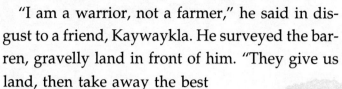

That night Geronimo sent several of his trusted warriors into the woods. "Follow the telegraph line," he said. "Find a place where it passes through a tree. Cut the line. Then tie the ends together with rawhide. That way no one will know where it has been cut. They won't be able to send any messages. We will have more time to escape."

THE next day, May 17, 1885, Geronimo and about 40 men and 90 women and children mounted horses and slipped out of the reservation. They rode as hard as they could toward their beloved Sierra Madre mountains, raiding as they went. They left a path of murdered settlers and burned buildings behind them.

When General Crook learned of Geronimo's escape, he summoned Apache guides and army troops to chase him. But this time Geronimo knew they would be coming and made extra efforts to hide his trail in the mountains. For almost a year Crook's Indian scouts and soldiers searched for the runaways without success.

Finally, in March 1886, Geronimo's followers persuaded him to meet with General Crook. They were tired of being constantly pursued. After talking for two days, Geronimo agreed to surrender on Crook's terms. His tribe would be sent to live on a reservation in Florida. After two years

there, they could return to the San Carlos reservation in Arizona.

But as they camped, Geronimo began to have doubts.

"You're being led into a trap," a trader told him. "As soon as you cross the border, they'll murder all of you."

Fearing the worst, Geronimo fled into the rainy night with 20 warriors and 18 women and children. He would make one last desperate attempt at freedom.

In April, General Crook, frustrated by Geronimo's escape and problems with his commanding officers, went back to Washington. General Nelson Miles assumed command. His first decision was to send all Chiricahua away from San Carlos. They were exiled to Florida.

Then General Miles spread his 5,000 troops throughout the region. For five long months he tried to trap Geronimo's little band of 38 Indians. But Geronimo was more mobile than ever. He even made daring raids into Arizona.

"We're not having much success trapping those renegades," General Miles remarked to Lieutenant Gatewood. "I want you to try something different. Take just a few men and find him. Then negotiate with him. He trusts you."

Lieutenant Gatewood rode through the Sierra Madre, listening for news. One day he found some Chiricahua women in the Mexican town of Fronteras, buying supplies. Quietly, he and a few men followed the women up into the mountains.

From high above, Geronimo observed them. "Tell Gatewood to come up alone," he ordered one of his braves.

Geronimo was tired. He knew his people wanted rest. "What will the U.S. government offer us if we give up?" he asked.

"I am only authorized to accept an unconditional surrender," Gatewood replied. "You and your people will be sent to Florida."

Geronimo scowled and drew himself up to his full height. "Take us back to San Carlos, or we will fight," he demanded.

"It would do you no good to return to San Carlos. The Chiricahua have already been sent to Florida," Gatewood said.

Geronimo stood in shocked silence. Hopelessness overwhelmed him. His people had no home. The Sierra Madre mountains were no longer safe. The Apaches didn't even have the reservation in Arizona. They had been expelled from their tribal lands. Geronimo bowed his head. His stubborn independence seemed to disappear.

"I will speak to General Miles," he said quietly.

ON September 4, 1886, Geronimo gave up the fight for his beloved way of life. He gave one last, sorrowful look across the mountains. "When Usen created the Apaches, he also created their homes in the West. Now we have no home. Once I moved about like the wind. Now I surrender to you and that is all."

And so the last great Apache warrior sadly turned himself over to the United States Army.

SKIDMORE COLLEGE LIBRARY

Joseph McCoy
Cattle Baron

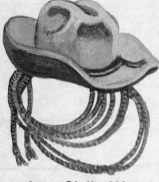

I've always loved solving problems. And believe me, there are plenty of big problems that need solving right now. We just got through fighting the Civil War, and the economy's in terrible shape. No one has any money. Yet there must be a way to get the economy back on its feet. This land has so many resources. If only I could think of something.

J OSEPH McCoy stood under an oak tree in the spring of 1867 and stared out across the Texas landscape.

"Look at those longhorns," he muttered.

All around him, longhorn cattle grazed in the high prairie grass. They were tall, lean animals with magnificent horns. They roamed freely over the fertile plains of Texas.

"It's a shame somebody can't make money off these animals," McCoy said to his friend Willie Sugg. "They aren't worth $5 a head here in Texas. But back in the East, people are clamoring for steak dinners. I bet longhorns would bring $40 a head in New York or Chicago."

"Yeah," Sugg agreed. "Too bad it's such a long

way to New York. Besides, there's no way to get 'em from here to the East."

"Don't be so sure," McCoy said thoughtfully, rubbing the goatee on his chin.

"Why? What are you planning to do? Send 'em back East in a parlor car?" Sugg chuckled at the idea.

"Why not?" asked McCoy.

"Well, for one thing, it's at least 600 or 700 miles from here to the railroads in Kansas," Sugg replied. "The only way to get a herd up there would be to drive 'em. Yes, sir, you'd have to drive 'em the whole way!"

"Well, then," said McCoy in a quiet but decisive voice, "I reckon that's just what I'll do."

"Don't be a fool!" scoffed Sugg. "You'd never get longhorns to Kansas! They're the most temperamental creatures on the face of this earth. It doesn't take more than a horsefly to make 'em stampede. Why, you'd be lucky to have a single one left at the end of the journey."

"I don't know," McCoy said. "I bet there are some experienced trail bosses who could handle a herd of ornery longhorns."

"Listen, Joe. Suppose someone were interested. Think of all the other dangers … flash floods, hailstorms, angry farmers, Indian raids, droughts …"

McCoy didn't answer. He was lost in thought. The idea of shipping Texas cattle to the East had captured his imagination. And once Joe McCoy took hold of an idea, he didn't quit until he had turned it into a reality.

"Somehow I'll make it work," he resolved. "It may take tremendous effort, but it'll be worth it. By the time I'm done, people from Chicago to Boston will be eating Texas beef every night of the week! And I'll be rich!"

OVER the next few weeks, McCoy worked on the details of his plan night and day.

"So far, everything is going smoothly," he wrote to his brother in Illinois. "I've struck a deal with the Union Pacific Railroad. They'll take the cattle east, and I'll give them all my business. I'm even building a brand new cattle town in Kansas — Abilene — right on the railroad line. I'm putting in a stockyard, feedlots, a hotel, a bank — the works! Pretty soon I'll have 100 cowboys bringing in 35,000 head of cattle. Abilene will be a real cow town before very long. Just wait and see!"

McCoy hired agents to spread the word about Abilene among the Texas cattle ranchers.

"Tell 'em I'll have buyers lined up and waiting," he directed the agents. "Tell 'em we have the most modern equipment around. Why, we can

load forty boxcars of cattle in two hours," he declared.

"Shanghai" Pierce, an experienced trail boss, was one of the first Texans to show interest.

"I bet if I got some good men and a nice, big herd of longhorns, I could really turn a buck," he mused. "Buyers lined up, guaranteed railroad passage … what could go wrong?"

But Shanghai knew plenty could go wrong on the 700-mile trail between San Antonio and Abilene. He knew that his most important task would be finding the right trail hands.

"I need a special breed of men. Men who are tough, honest, and fearless," he announced in every Texas town from Fort Worth to San Antonio. "Above all, I need men who won't quit halfway up the trail. I've got to have men who can handle trouble."

Cowhands took the job offer as a challenge and jumped at the chance to prove their mettle.

BY June, Shanghai Pierce and about thirty other cowboys had set out for the long drive up the Chisholm Trail. The first few days of the

drive were backbreaking. The jumpy longhorns were difficult to control. The cowhands pushed them hard, 25 or 30 miles a day, to tire them out. Once they were off their range, they were easier to handle.

The long hours on the trail took their toll on the men. They headed out before dawn, and sometimes kept driving long after sunset.

"When are we gonna quit for the day?" a cowboy called to Shanghai one day, after riding twenty hours without sleep.

"Gotta keep going until we find water for the cattle," Shanghai replied curtly.

By midnight, however, it seemed clear that there wasn't any water to be found.

"Okay," called Shanghai. "Pack it in. We'll stop here for a few hours and get some sleep. I'm posting guards to watch the animals since they've been restless all day. They'll be more likely to stampede in the dark. I just hope the weather holds out, and we don't get a thunderstorm."

Shanghai decided he would take the first night shift himself. He asked Rick Wheeler to join him. As the other men drifted off to sleep, Rick and Shanghai slumped in their saddles, listening to the sounds of the night. In the distance a coyote howled. A few of the cattle began to stir.

TO calm them and shut out the disturbing noises, Rick began to sing.

"O say, li'l dogies, when you goin' to lay down,
And give up this driftin' and rovin' around?
My horse is leg-weary and I'm awful tired,
But if you get away, I'm sure to be fired.
Lay down, little dogies, lay down."

Shanghai rubbed the back of his neck. It was stiff from so many hours on the trail. His mind wandered to his family back in San Antonio. He missed them.

Just then lightning flashed in the distance.

"Uh, oh," exclaimed Shanghai. "It looks like trouble!" Sure enough, the cattle began moving restlessly. Several more bolts of lightning stung the sky, one right after the other. Thunder exploded like a cannonshot. Half a dozen spooked cattle took off. In eerie silence the rest of the herd followed in a mad charge.

"Stampede! Up and at 'em!" Shanghai yelled to the sleeping trail hands.

The men grabbed their blankets and ran for their horses, dreading the coming ordeal. Then they rode at a full gallop for three or four miles.

Spike and Nelson, the fastest riders, spurred their mares to get in front of the herd. They tried to "mill" the cattle — get them to run in a circle.

"Watch out!" Nelson cautioned his young companion.

This was the most dangerous time for the trail hands. Crowded between the frantic animals, a man could easily be knocked off his horse. If that happened, he would probably be trampled to death.

Finally, the exhausted cattle slowed to a trot, then to a weary walk.

"That was close!" Spike exclaimed in relief, grateful that he had lived through his first stampede.

"Looks like we've lost quite a few cows," Shanghai grumbled.

"Could've been worse, boss," Nelson commented, after all the men were accounted for. "Could have been lots worse."

As the weeks passed, the cattle became calmer and less likely to stampede. But the trail hands faced other hardships. They had to wait a week to cross the Red River, which was swollen with rain. One man was almost drowned as his horse was swept downstream.

Angry farmers demanded money before they would permit the herd to cross their farms. As Shanghai dug in his pocket to pay the second "crossing fee" that day, he thought of McCoy.

"I sure hope things are going more smoothly in Abilene than they are out here," he muttered irritably.

FINALLY, after ten hard weeks on the trail, Shanghai and his men drove the herd into Abilene, Kansas. Joseph McCoy had seen to it that preparations were indeed going smoothly. But he had grown anxious waiting for the herd. When he saw them coming, he whooped with excitement.

"Look!" he cried to the hired hands in his new stockyard. "Here they come! Here come the first Texas longhorns to make it to Abilene!"

McCoy rushed up to shake Shanghai's hand.

"So it *is* possible!" he said, glowing with excitement and relief. "I knew it could be done!"

"Oh, it's possible all right," replied Shanghai wryly. "It just ain't easy. I sure hope those Easterners appreciate these steak dinners!"

"Oh, they'll appreciate them," replied McCoy. "And they'll make us rich men to show their gratitude!"

ANNIE OAKLEY
A SHOOTING STAR

I'm small and petite. But because of my peculiar talent, people who have never met me expect me to be big and blustering and mean and threatening. They are usually surprised by my sweet, gentle manner and quiet voice. No one ever tries to threaten me, though. I never have to worry about that!

PHOEBE Anne Oakley Mozee followed her stepfather through the gray November woods. The leaves crunched beneath her feet as she hurried to keep up with him.

"I sure hope we get a turkey for Thanksgiving," she thought.

As the hours passed, Annie grew discouraged. There didn't seem to be any gobblers in the woods near Greenville, Ohio, for this 1867 holiday. Annie's mind began to wander. She wished she were old enough to go hunting on her own, instead of just tagging along with her stepfather.

"Pa?" she whispered.

"Yes?" her stepfather responded.

"Do you think I could learn to shoot a gun someday?"

"You?" He laughed. "Why, Annie, you're no bigger than a bird yourself. You're only seven years old. The kick from a gun would knock you clean off your feet."

"No it wouldn't, Pa. I bet I'd be a good shot."

Her stepfather grinned. "Well," he said, "let's find out. Here, you take my gun and see what you can hit."

He gave her the gun and showed her how to aim it. She held the butt of the rifle against her shoulder and put her eye to the sight. Suddenly,

she and her stepfather heard the squawking call of a wild turkey.

"Give me the gun!" her stepfather whispered.

But Annie held it tight, peering through the trees for a glimpse of the turkey. She felt her heart thumping with excitement. At last she spotted it — a big, dark turkey in the bushes fifty yards away. Without stopping to think, Annie took aim and pulled the trigger. The gun roared, and a great puff of black smoke flew out of the rifle. The force of the blast sent Annie reeling backwards. When the smoke cleared and she regained her balance, she saw her stepfather running toward the fallen bird.

"I can't believe it!" he cried. "Annie, you shot this bird right through the head — a perfect hit! None of the meat will be spoiled!"

The next day, during Thanksgiving dinner, Annie's stepfather raved about her ability.

"I'm telling you, Suzanne," he said to Annie's mother, "this girl's a natural. She shot a bull's-eye the first time she fired a gun!"

Annie glowed with pride at the compliment. From then on, her stepfather often let her go hunting with him. Sometimes he would hand her the rifle and let her try her aim on a squirrel, a rabbit, or a quail. She never missed. And she always shot her game cleanly, right through the head.

ANNIE loved hunting with her stepfather. But the outings ended with his death the following year. The Mozee family was plunged into poverty. Annie's mother had no money to pay the mortgage or buy food.

"Don't worry, Ma," Annie said bravely. "I'll help out."

The next day she took her stepfather's rifle down from the fireplace mantle. She filled the powder horn with gunpowder, and put some caps and bullets in her pocket. Then she walked out into the woods. For an hour she moved stealthily through the forest, looking for game. At last she spied the mottled brown feathers of a quail. Instantly she raised the gun to her shoulder, took aim, and fired. The quail dropped. Once again, she had made a clean hit. All day Annie roamed the woods with her stepfather's rifle looking for game. By late afternoon, she had filled her sack with quail.

"Ma!" she called as she ran toward the cabin. "Ma, I've got enough quail for supper, and much more besides!"

The next morning, Annie took the extra game to Katzenberger's General Store.

"Mr. Katzenberger, do you know of anyone who would be interested in buying fresh quail?" she asked.

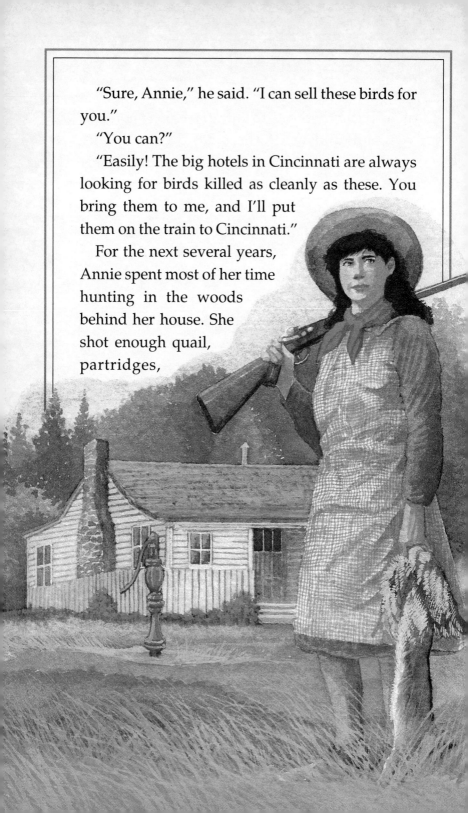

"Sure, Annie," he said. "I can sell these birds for you."

"You can?"

"Easily! The big hotels in Cincinnati are always looking for birds killed as cleanly as these. You bring them to me, and I'll put them on the train to Cincinnati."

For the next several years, Annie spent most of her time hunting in the woods behind her house. She shot enough quail, partridges, and turkeys to feed her family. She sold the extra game to Mr. Katzenberger. She made so much money that she was able to pay off the entire mortgage on her family's home.

By the time Annie turned fifteen, everyone in Darke County had heard of her. She had gained a reputation as the best shot in the county.

"How do you do it, Annie?" people asked her again and again.

She always shrugged and gave them the same answer. "I don't know. I just wait until it feels right, then I pull the trigger."

IN November 1875, Annie visited her sister in Cincinnati. There she heard about a shooting match to be held on Thanksgiving Day. It sounded like fun, and her sister encouraged her to enter.

Her opponent was Frank Butler, a professional marksman who had his own traveling show. When he saw the 90-pound Annie getting ready for the match, he broke into a wide grin.

"Don't tell me you're going to compete against me," he said with a merry twinkle in his eye.

"Why not?" Annie answered him shyly.

"Well," he said with another grin, "just let me warn you: I'm pretty good."

"Well, so am I," Annie thought to herself.

Annie had never competed in a match before. In this match, the contestants had to shoot round clay targets, called pigeons, that were thrown into the air one at a time. Each contestant had to shoot at 25 targets. The person who hit the most pigeons won.

Frank went first. Confidently he shot down target after target, missing only one. Then it was Annie's turn. She stepped nervously up to the shooting circle and waited for the first pigeon. Even though her heart was pounding, her hands stayed steady. When the target sailed across her sight, she took careful aim and fired. The clay target shattered. Before she knew it, she had hit all 25 pigeons.

"And the winner is ... Miss Annie Mozee!" cried the announcer.

Annie beamed. She looked over at her opponent, Frank Butler, and was amazed to see him smiling, too.

"Congratulations, Miss Mozee," he said, walking over to shake her hand. "I have to say you're the best sharpshooter I've ever seen — even if you are a young lady."

Annie just smiled.

"May I help you celebrate by taking you to dinner?" he asked.

Annie nodded. She was fascinated by this tall, good-natured Irishman.

BY the following spring, Annie and Frank were deeply in love. On June 22, 1876, they were married. Frank wanted Annie to perform in his traveling show, but she was not interested.

For several months, Frank continued to perform with his partner, Billy Graham, while Annie watched from the audience. One day, however, Billy became ill and could not perform.

"Annie," Frank pleaded, "will you please fill in for Billy? Just this once?"

"All right, Frank," she said. "I'll give it a try."

That night Annie stepped onto a stage for the first time in her life. When the audience saw the four-foot-eleven-inch lady walk onto the stage, they gasped. A hush fell over them as they waited to see what this pretty young woman could do.

Annie closed her eyes and imagined that she was out in the woods in Greenville. Then she opened her eyes and took aim at a bottle at the other end of the stage. She neatly blew the cork out of it.

The audience cheered. Annie smiled shyly and did more tricks. She shot out a candle flame. She threw five glass balls in the air, and shot them all before they hit the ground. Then, she asked for a volunteer from the audience. A man stepped up, and Annie handed him a penny.

"Hold this straight out at your side," she instructed him.

While the man shut his eyes in fear, she shot the penny right out of his hand.

The crowd jumped up, cheering wildly. Annie smiled and waved. She felt she would burst with pride and happiness.

To Frank's delight, Annie became a regular on the show. She took the stage name "Annie Oakley." She and Frank performed in cities all across America. Annie Oakley was becoming a famous celebrity. Frank decided to stop performing and become her manager. With her husband's support, Annie's skill neared perfection.

IN 1885 Annie became a member of the Buffalo Bill Wild West show. She performed all kinds of outrageous stunts. She threw five glass balls into the air, turned a handspring, then shot all the balls before they hit the ground. She sliced the thin edge of a playing card with a bullet from 90 feet. She stood on a galloping horse and shot the flames from a turning wheel of candles. She shot cigarettes from the mouths of audience volunteers. Another member of the cast, Chief Sitting Bull, nicknamed her "Little Sure Shot."

By the late 1880's, Annie Oakley had become a national sensation. The petite girl from Ohio amazed people with her grace and ability. The world had never seen a sharpshooter with her accuracy, talent, and style.

Jane Addams
Founder of Hull House

I had a dream when I was a girl living in a small town in Illinois. I dreamed that I had a big house. It was surrounded by tiny houses. The doors of the big house were always open. People could go there for help. They could find food, warmth, shelter, and understanding.

I wonder if my dream will come true. I want so badly to do something useful with my life.

JANE Addams walked across the campus of the Woman's Medical College in Philadelphia in the spring of 1882. Suddenly, a sharp pain shot through her back. She felt dizzy and faint. Then, as another stab of pain pierced her back, she fell to the ground.

She was rushed to the hospital. There doctors realized that curvature of the spine had damaged her spinal column.

"Your spine is very weak now," one doctor told her, "and cannot support the weight of your body. I'm afraid you may have to spend the rest of your life in bed."

"But that's impossible!" cried Jane. "I'm going

to be a doctor! I have to be able to walk and move around."

"I'm sorry," the doctor said. "But I don't think you'll be able to finish medical school now."

Jane felt crushed. For months she lay in bed in a state of depression. She wouldn't read, and she wouldn't talk to anyone. She barely ate enough to stay alive. At last, in desperation, her stepbrother decided to operate. He was a skilled surgeon.

"Of course surgery on the spine is very dangerous," he told her. "But if the operation is successful, there's a chance you will be able to walk again."

Jane was thrilled. She had hope again for a new life. The operation was a long and delicate one. And for months afterward she had to do special exercises. These were extremely painful, but Jane never complained. Finally, her hard work was rewarded. She was able to walk again.

Jane's family had plenty of money. As part of her recovery, she traveled to Europe with a friend from college, Ellen Gates Starr. There she took music lessons and learned German, French, and Italian. She went to galleries, theaters, and museums. Jane enjoyed these activities, but she was not entirely happy. She felt that something vital was missing from her life.

"This is not the kind of life I want to live," she told Ellen. "I feel so useless. When I graduated from college, I thought I would be able to do something important with my skills."

ONE afternoon in 1888, Jane visited a part of London that would change her life. She went to Whitechapel district, the poorest section of the city. There, amid the dirt and poverty, she saw a tall, well-kept building called Toynbee Hall. It seemed out of place among the poor dwellings around it. Filled with curiosity, Jane knocked on the door.

"Excuse me," she said to the young man who opened the door, "could you tell me something about this place?"

"We're a 'settlement house,'" he explained. "A group of us came here after college and settled in the neighborhood. We live here, among the poor, and do what we can to help them."

Jane felt a stirring in her heart that she hadn't felt since medical school. Perhaps *this* was the kind of work she could do. She hurried back to her hotel and told Ellen about it.

"I've made a big decision. I'm going back to America and open my own settlement house," she declared excitedly. "Do you want to help me?"

Ellen was uncertain at first, but she was soon swept up in Jane's enthusiasm. In January 1889, the two women went to Chicago, determined to help others. They walked bravely into the nineteenth ward, the poorest slum in the city.

"This is terrible," Ellen whispered to Jane as they walked down Polk Avenue. "I had no idea that people lived like this."

Indeed, they were shocked by the poverty and despair they saw everywhere. Garbage lay strewn along the sidewalks. Little children ran barefoot through streets littered with pieces of broken glass. The buildings sagged with old and rotten wood.

And in many alleys and doorways, people stood huddled against the cold. Some of them wrapped their hands and feet in newspapers for warmth.

"This is where we must settle," said Jane as an old woman approached her, begging for food. "This is where we are needed most."

AS Jane stood there, still with a slight hunch to her back, she glanced at the intersection of Polk and South Halsted Street. There, on the corner, stood a run-down old mansion.

"Look," she called to Ellen, "what about that big old house? There's a 'For Rent' sign in the window."

"Are you sure this is the place you want?" Ellen asked hesitantly. "It's a wreck!"

"This is the place," said Jane firmly. "This is where I want to settle. I know we can help the people here."

That afternoon Jane and Ellen visited the rental agency and asked about the old mansion. The agent stared at the two well-dressed young women in amazement.

"That's the old Charles Hull place," he said. "In Mr. Hull's day, it was beautiful. But now it's a mess, full of trash and filth. Besides, it's in the middle of the immigrant neighborhood. The people moved there from Germany, Italy, Russia, Poland, and Greece. The area is very poor. Surely you can't be serious about renting a house there."

Jane dismissed his words with one wave of her hand.

"Here's the money for the first month's rent," she said.

For the next several months, Jane poured her energy into Hull House. She called on many wealthy families in Chicago and asked them for donations.

Few people could turn down the charming Miss Addams. She disarmed them with her soft voice, frail appearance, and determined spirit. Soon Jane collected enough money to give Hull House a solid financial base.

THROUGHOUT the summer of 1889, workers rebuilt walls and put on a new roof. They installed running water and brought in new furniture. By September, Hull House shone with fresh paint, newly scrubbed bricks, and clean windows. On September 18, Jane, Ellen, and a housekeeper named Mary Keyser moved in and formally opened the first settlement house in the United States. Then Jane set out down the street to meet her new neighbors.

Opening the door of a German bakery, she was greeted by the warm smell of freshly baked rolls.

"Guten Morgen," she called out loudly.

The baker seemed surprised to hear Jane use his native tongue. He rushed over and began talking to her. Jane explained who she was and why she was there. Then she listened as the baker explained what life was like in this neighborhood.

"None of my customers speak English," he told her. "They are all Germans, like me. Most were farmers back in the old country. Life is hard for them in this strange city. They have very little

education and speak no English, so they can't get decent jobs. They work twelve to fourteen hours a day in factories and earn only a few pennies."

Jane shuddered. She could imagine how hopeless life seemed to these poor people. How disappointed they must be with their new lives in the United States.

"Will you do me a favor?" she asked the baker. "Will you please tell your customers about Hull House? Tell them they are welcome to visit anytime. We will help them learn English. We will give them sewing lessons or reading lessons or whatever else we can. And tell them never to go to bed hungry. They can always get a meal at Hull House."

The baker promised to spread the word. Jane thanked him, then moved on to the other immigrant neighborhoods in the nineteenth ward. By the end of the day, she had covered many blocks and talked to dozens of people.

That night, as she sat in the Hull House parlor, Jane felt the old stinging pain in her back. Tears welled in her eyes as she struggled to her feet.

"I can't let a little pain stop me from doing my work," she thought with determination. She recalled the day the doctor had told her that she would spend the rest of her life in bed. "I will never let myself sink into such a state of depression again," she vowed. "I don't have time for self-pity. There is too much I want to do. There are too many people who need help."

FOR the next few weeks, however, only a few people came to Hull House. Most were curious onlookers who had no intention of becoming involved in the settlement house. But Jane and Ellen were so kind and so gracious to these people that they kept coming back. Slowly they overcame their fear and joined fully in the activities of Hull House.

That first year, Ellen taught a reading class for Italian women. Jane started a kindergarten for local children. Hull House also set up a day care center and a boy's club to keep gangs off the streets. Hull House became a cultural center, offering adult classes in health, art, and music. Special Old World festivities, like Russian folk dances and special Polish dinners, were celebrated there. In addition, hot meals were offered to anyone who needed them.

The work load often seemed overwhelming, but still Jane and Ellen kept adding programs. Jane was very successful at recruiting volunteers to help run the new programs.

As Jane watched the people pouring into Hull House, she felt pleased with its success.

"Hull House is my dream house. When people enter its doors, hope enters their lives. They know they can come here for help and understanding. In a small but important way, I feel that Hull House has made a difference in the lives of everyone who comes here."

F.E. AND F.O. STANLEY

INVENTORS OF THE STANLEY STEAMER

I'm F.E. and he's F.O. We're twins. We've been hearing about this new-fangled thing called a "horseless carriage." We want to try to build one, too. But ours will be the *best*. We'll build one that can speed along at ten miles per hour! And it will look great, too.

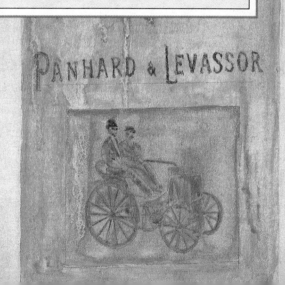

PANHARD & LEVASSOR

LADIES and gentlemen! Step right up! Come see the Marvel of the Age!" the attendant barked out his invitation. "Hurry, hurry, hurry! The demonstration will begin in just a few minutes!"

Tickets in hand, a set of identical twins named Francis Edgar Stanley and Freelan Oscar Stanley rushed toward the brightly colored tent. The two men, nicknamed F.E. and F.O., couldn't wait to see the horseless carriage. It had come all the way from France to the 1896 Maine fair.

"I wonder what this machine can do," whispered F.E. to his twin.

Inside the tent, the brothers sat quietly while a man fired up the boiler on the horseless carriage. The carriage began to shake. A snorting cough came from its engine. The man climbed in and opened the throttle. Suddenly the carriage lurched forward. It was actually moving!

Powered only by steam, the carriage jolted its way across the stage. Before it reached the other side, the engine sputtered and stalled. Most people were thrilled to have seen the "Marvel of the Age" move even a few feet. What a change from the horse and buggy! Only a few tough customers, like Francis and Freelan, remained unimpressed.

"I didn't think that contraption was so marvel-
ous," grumbled F.O. afterwards. "Did you?"

"No," said F.E. "Why, I bet we could build a
better model ourselves."

F.E. and his brother loved tinkering on new
projects and inventions. They had already made
violins by hand and developed a new dry photo-
graphic process. Building a steam-powered car
would be another great project for their energies.

Eagerly the brothers went to work on what
would become their very first "Stanley Steamer."

The twins used the seats and body of a regular horse-drawn carriage. Under the floorboards they installed a twenty-gallon water tank. They connected that to a boiler, a kerosene burner, and a two-cylinder engine. Although the engine was small, it was incredibly powerful and efficient. The whole thing contained fewer than 26 moving parts — each one carefully crafted by the Stanley brothers.

"Look at it," F.E. said, glowing with delight as he put the finishing touches on the vehicle. "Just look at it!"

"It's a real beauty," admitted the ever-practical F.O. "But will it work?"

They fired up the boiler. When the water had heated to boiling, they heard the faint whistle of steam building up in the engine.

As F.O. held his breath, F.E. opened the throttle. Without a sound, the carriage began to move forward.

"We did it! We did it!" the twins shouted together.

Brimming with pride, they drove the Steamer along the winding dirt roads of Lewiston, Maine. They said little, simply enjoying the eerie silence of their new machine as it rolled down the road.

The brothers were hooked. They built several more models, adding improvements to the original design. In 1898, they entered their Steamer in an automobile race. The Steamer won! It also finished first in a hill-climbing contest.

S OON the Stanley brothers began to make Steamers to sell to others. In 1899, they opened the Stanley Motor Carriage Company in a factory in Newton, Massachusetts. They made two hundred Steamers that first year, and sold every one.

People came from all over the New England area as word spread of this new moving contraption. F.E. and F.O. personally interviewed each potential buyer. They wouldn't sell a Steamer to anyone who didn't meet their standards.

The Stanley brothers also weeded out customers by charging a high price for their cars. In 1916, a Stanley Steamer cost about $2,500. That was a large sum of money in those days — and the brothers demanded cash on the spot. They didn't sell on credit.

Customers who passed all the tests were permitted to buy a Stanley Steamer. Then one of the brothers gave them a personal introduction to their new car.

"Here is your Stanley Steamer," F.E. said to a proud new owner, Max Smith.

"I'm so excited!" said Max. "I've been looking forward to this for months. Is it true what they say about the power in these Steamers? Can they really go through a brick wall?"

"Yes, they're amazing machines, all right," F.E. said. "I can see that you're eager to learn to drive one. First you have to light the kerosene burner." He struck a match and adjusted the knob. Nothing happened. "Sometimes it's a little hard to light," he explained.

After using up half a box of kitchen matches, F.E. finally succeeded in lighting the burner.

"Now you have to wait for the water in the boiler to reach the right temperature for a good head of steam. You can check these gauges here," F.E. said, pointing to a row of gauges by the driver's seat. "It usually takes about thirty minutes. That's about the same amount of time you'd spend hitching up the horse and buggy."

W HEN the engine was finally ready, F.E. invited Max to drive.

"Just pull back easy on the throttle," he said. "If you want to go slow, leave the throttle open a tiny bit. But if it's speed you want, go ahead and open it up all the way. But watch out! These things can go from zero to sixty in eleven seconds!"

"I'll just take it easy for now," said Max, easing the throttle open until they were cruising at twenty miles per hour.

"See those pedals on the floor?" asked F.E. "The one on the right is for the brake, and the one on the left is for reverse. You know, a Steamer can go as fast backwards as it can forwards."

"Great!" said Max. "I'd love to race this against my neighbor's new gas-powered car. I bet I could beat him going backwards!"

Then several dogs began to chase the car, barking and howling as they ran beside it.

"What do you suppose is the matter with those dogs?" asked Max.

"Oh, they're just howling because of the sound," replied F.E.

"What sound? This vehicle doesn't make a sound. It's quiet as can be," said Max, puzzled.

"It's a high-pitched sound that only dogs can hear. Pull that steamboat whistle — that'll discourage them from chasing us," F.E. instructed.

"Driving a Stanley Steamer is certainly an adventure," Max commented.

SUDDENLY a flame three feet long shot out from the side of the Steamer.

"We're on fire!" screamed Max, slamming on the brake.

"It's all right," said F.E. calmly. "It's just the fuel burner. Sometimes it floods. Turn that knob to turn off the kerosene supply. The fire will burn itself out in a minute."

The fire soon died down to a thin trickle of smoke.

"As I was saying," said Max, "driving a Stanley Steamer is certainly an adventure."

"Well, you don't have to worry about that fire problem. The riding area is fireproof. If an onlooker panics, though, and puts the fire out with water, you might get a little wet," F.E. said, chuckling.

When the demonstration drive was over, F.E. shook Max's hand. "I hope you like your Stanley Steamer," he said. "You take care of it, and it will take you anywhere you want to go."

I N 1899, F.O. decided to see exactly where the Stanley Steamer could go. So he headed for Mount Washington, the tallest peak in New England. He steered the Steamer up the winding rutted wagon trail. It chugged quietly the ten miles to the top.

"I'm the first person ever to drive a car up that mountain," F.O. bragged to his friends. "And it took only two hours and ten minutes."

Three years later, though, a gasoline-powered car heaved itself up the same mountain — and beat F.O.'s record by ten minutes.

F.O. scowled when he heard the news.

"I'll tell you what," F.E. said to him. "We've made quite a few improvements in our carriage in the last three years. And I'm going to prove once and for all that our new product is the best, the fastest, and the most durable vehicle on the road."

With that, F.E. drove the new model of the Steamer up Mount Washington in 27 minutes.

As word of this accomplishment spread, people everywhere had to agree with F.E. The Stanley Steamer *was* the best car around. And if further proof was needed, the Stanley Brothers supplied it in 1906. On January 26, at the Ormond-Daytona Tournament of Speed in Florida, the Stanleys entered their newest model in a race. Called the

Stanley Rocket, it shattered the previous world speed record. The Stanley Rocket flew down the beach at 127 miles per hour. The driver, Fred Marriott, became the first person to go faster than two miles per minute.

Orders for Steamers filled the brothers' office. Their friends praised their skills and envied their newfound fame.

"You must be pleased with the large number of orders. It seems that everyone in America wants a Steamer," commented one customer.

"Making a fortune has never been our goal in this business," F.E. replied. "Our goal has been to build the finest automobile possible for ourselves. If someone else wants one, that's fine, too. We won't compromise our standards by advertising or mass-producing our cars. Each Stanley Steamer is made individually and personally checked by one of us. Each one is unique and serves as its own advertisement. There is no better car made than the Stanley Steamer."

WILLIAM GORGAS
CONQUEROR OF YELLOW FEVER

I'm a doctor, a scientist. I know what causes yellow fever and how to stop it. But I need support. Why won't any of the officials in Washington respond? This is a matter of life and death. America is committed to completing the Panama Canal. But there will be no canal if this deadly fever continues. Yellow fever will destroy our great plan.

DR. William Gorgas stood in the middle of the jungle in Colón, Panama, in June 1904. Even here, in the shade of the trees, the temperature was a sweltering 98 degrees. Dr. Gorgas heard the jungle birds screeching and the swamp frogs croaking. He could feel his skin itching as dozens of mosquitoes plunged their stingers into his neck and arms. They were always in the air — attacking and biting.

"So this is where we're going to build a canal, eh?" he said to his guide.

The guide nodded. "President Roosevelt is determined, sir. He says he wants to see the dirt fly here on the Isthmus. Building a canal across Panama will be good for trade. It will take boats much less time to get from the Atlantic Ocean to the Pacific Ocean."

Dr. Gorgas ran his hand through his smooth white hair. "Yes," he said thoughtfully. "The French said the same thing. For nearly ten years they tried to build a canal here so ships wouldn't have to sail all the way around South America. But every year one-third of the French workers died of yellow fever. The human cost of building a canal was too high. Too many men died from the fever. Finally the French abandoned the idea."

"Well, sir, isn't your job to get rid of the yellow fever?"

Dr. Gorgas gave a grim little smile. "Yes," he said solemnly. "That is my mission. And if I fail, President Roosevelt's canal project will fail, too. No canal project can succeed until the threat of yellow fever is eliminated."

As he settled into his office in Colón, Panama, Dr. Gorgas sighed. There was so much to be done! And he needed so many things! He knew it would take a tremendous effort to get rid of yellow fever. Quickly he wrote out a request for supplies and took it to John Wallace, chief engineer for the canal project.

"What's this?" grunted Wallace as he read the request form. "Eight *tons* of insect powder? Ten thousand yards of porch screening? One hundred tons of sulphur?"

"Well, sir, that is a preliminary estimate of my needs. Of course I might find that I need more as I begin to —"

"You must be out of your mind!" bellowed Wallace angrily. "Listen here, Gorgas. You're here as sanitary engineer. That means you're supposed to clean up this swamp. Get rid of the garbage. Get rid of the rats. Don't waste my time and money with these ridiculous requests!"

"But, sir," Dr. Gorgas protested. "I need these supplies to drive away the mosquitoes that cause yellow fever."

"Mosquitoes don't cause yellow fever!" shouted Wallace. "Rats and dirt and garbage cause it!"

"You're wrong, sir," Dr. Gorgas persisted. "Four years ago scientists found that *Stegomyia* mosquitoes are the real enemy. When these mosquitoes bite people who have yellow fever, they pick up infected blood. Then when they bite healthy people, they pass on the infection. The only way to get rid of yellow fever is to get rid of the *Stegomyia* mosquitoes." Dr. Gorgas paused. "Please, sir, sign my requests for supplies. I'll prove to you that I am right."

"No," said Wallace firmly.

Dr. Gorgas sighed. "Well," he said softly, "then

I'll send my requests to Washington without your approval."

"Go ahead," scoffed Wallace. "Nobody's going to listen. No one will give you money for such foolish items."

A S the weeks went by, Dr. Gorgas found that John Wallace was right. None of the officials in Washington believed mosquitoes caused the deadly yellow fever. No one cared about the scientific evidence. They still clung to the old notion that the disease was caused by filth.

"Why don't you just get busy sweeping the streets?" the officials urged. "Pick up the garbage, whitewash the buildings. Don't waste your time with pesky little mosquitoes."

Dr. Gorgas became increasingly annoyed. Why wouldn't the leaders in Washington listen to him? He sent telegram after telegram pleading for help, but the supplies never came.

The American workers who were coming to the Canal Zone would not cooperate, either.

"Cover the rain barrels where you store your drinking water," Gorgas instructed them.

"Why, Doc?" asked one man. "What's the big deal?"

"*Stegomyia* mosquitoes lay their eggs in calm water. If we keep them from laying eggs, they will die out, and yellow fever will die out with them."

The men laughed. Like many others, they didn't believe that tiny mosquitoes could carry deadly diseases.

BY November 1904, Dr. Gorgas was very discouraged. He had accomplished nothing. There were now 3,500 American workers in Panama. He knew that sooner or later they would be plagued by an outbreak of yellow fever.

It happened even sooner than he had expected. On November 21, he saw the first case of yellow fever. The man's skin was turning yellow and his temperature was raging.

"It's Yellow Jack, isn't it, Doc?" the man asked in a moment of clarity.

Dr. Gorgas nodded. Then he ordered the man isolated from all other patients at the hospital. Over the next few months, dozens of men became sick with the dreaded disease. Dr. Gorgas cared for these patients himself. He had survived an attack of yellow fever years earlier. His body now had immunity to fight off the disease, so he was in no danger of catching it again.

All through the winter, Dr. Gorgas quietly treated yellow fever victims. He didn't publicize the growing number of cases because he didn't want the canal workers to panic. The following spring, however, the word leaked out. Newspaper headlines trumpeted the news: "YELLOW JACK IN PANAMA!"

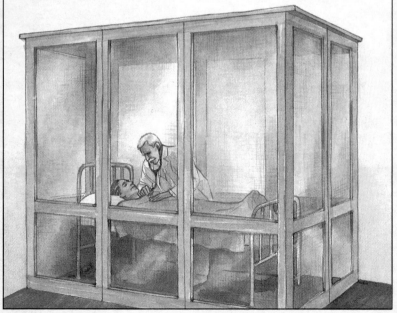

Canal workers became terrified. Suddenly they all wanted to leave Panama. Dr. Gorgas watched in dismay as they flocked to the harbor, elbowing their way onto boats headed back to the United States. Within a few weeks, three-fourths of all Americans in Panama had returned home.

In the midst of this mass desertion, John Wallace came to Dr. Gorgas's hut.

"I thought you should know that I'm leaving, too," he announced gruffly. "I've already notified President Roosevelt. I can't work under these conditions. It was madness to think we could build a canal through this jungle." Wallace paused. "And I'll tell you something else," he added in a bitter tone. "You were no help at all. You were paid to prevent an epidemic like this — and all you did was run around talking about mosquitoes!"

Dr. Gorgas knew there was no point in arguing. John Wallace would never understand medical research.

ON July 26, 1905, Wallace's replacement, John Stevens, arrived in Colón. Dr. Gorgas was waiting for him anxiously.

"Mr. Stevens, I don't mind telling you that you're my only hope," the doctor said to him. "If you support my efforts, I think we can still save the canal project."

As Gorgas explained about the yellow fever mosquitoes, he searched Stevens's face for some reaction. At last he finished speaking. He jammed his hands into his pockets and looked at Stevens anxiously. Would he help? Would he approve the necessary supplies?

"Well," said Stevens after a moment's silence, "I can see that we need to move quickly. Give me a complete list of the things you need. I'll send it on to Washington immediately."

Dr. Gorgas felt his heart soar with excitement. At last he had found someone who believed him. Rushing straight to his office, he wrote up the list.

He asked for $90,000 worth of screening, 3,000 garbage cans, 1,000 brooms, and 4,000 buckets. He asked for 300 tons of sulphur and 120 tons of insect powder. Finally, he requested enough money to hire 4,000 sanitation workers.

True to his promise, John Stevens forwarded the list to Washington. He demanded that officials send the materials. Soon Dr. Gorgas had everything he had ordered. He and his workers then began a house-by-house battle to kill the deadly mosquitoes. They sealed the cracks in every wall with newspaper and paste. They covered every window with wire screens.

"We've got to make sure mosquitoes don't get inside these buildings," Dr. Gorgas said. "If they get indoors, they'll find plenty of places to lay eggs — water glasses, bathtubs, sinks."

Dr. Gorgas and his workers also took Dutch ovens into every house. They filled the ovens with sulphur and let the sulphur burn for four hours. That killed any mosquitoes already indoors.

Outside, they cleared the streets of everything that could hold stagnant water. Tin cans, clay pots, curved pieces of glass — everything was swept up and put in covered garbage cans. Workers dug drainage ditches in the area to get rid of the swampy waters near the canal site.

Some swamps and ponds were too big to be drained. So Dr. Gorgas ordered workers to pour kerosene into them. The kerosene formed a film on the top of the water, killing all the mosquito eggs there. It took more than 50,000 gallons of kerosene each month for this project, but Dr. Gorgas managed to keep the swamps covered with oil. He was winning the war against yellow fever!

B Y October 1905, Dr. Gorgas had achieved amazing results. In less than three months, the *Stegomyia* mosquitoes had been driven out of the Canal Zone. Yellow fever had been stamped out! Work on the canal could proceed!

When the Panama Canal opened in 1914, Americans cheered. They applauded the 50-mile canal and the men who built it. Most people didn't realize that Dr. William Gorgas was the real hero of the project. With the support of John Stevens, he had eliminated yellow fever and made the Panama Canal possible.

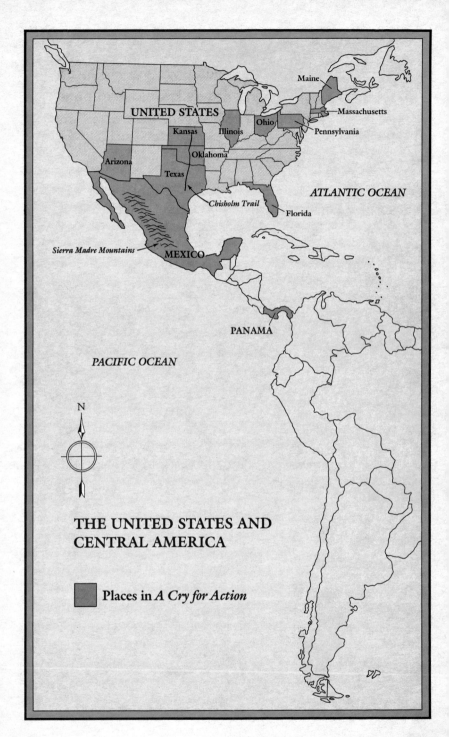

THE UNITED STATES AND
CENTRAL AMERICA

Places in *A Cry for Action*